Fika Fix

Your Life

With Coffee, People and Happiness

The Swedish ABCs of Feeling Good

Åsa Katarina Odbäck & Émile Odbäck Nelson

FikaFix.com

PEACEFUL VIKING BOOKS

ISBN: 9780692787830

Design by Åsa Katarina Odbäck & Émile Nelson
Art by Åsa Katarina Odbäck

AsaKatarina.com

Acknowledgements:

Thank you to all of the tireless researchers who compiled the data that allowed us to write this book, and an equally big thank you to all of the incredible people who have helped us along this journey. We are endlessly grateful to you all!

"I feel a very unusual sensation – it is not indigestion; I think it must be gratitude."
Benjamin Disraeli

Table of Contents

Coffee recipes and stories are sprinkled throughout the book, with a few Swedish cake and cookie recipes at the end. Enjoy it one sip at a time!

"Among the numerous luxuries of the table... coffee may be considered as one of the most valuable. It excites cheerfulness without intoxication; and the pleasing flow of spirits which it occasions...is never followed by sadness, languor or debility." *Benjamin Franklin*

"We get older, and we forget that we have to carve a little time out to feel good in your body, in your head, and in your spirit." *Estelle*

FIKA

"Swedes prefer not to translate the word fika. They don't want it to lose significance and become a mere coffee break... Fika is much more than having a coffee. It is a social phenomenon, a legitimate reason to set aside a moment for quality time. Fika can happen at any time, morning as well as evening. It can be savored at home, at work or in a café. It can be with colleagues, family, friends, or someone you are trying to get to know. It is a tradition observed frequently, preferably several times a day."
Sweden.se

(Pronounced: Fee-kah)

"A cup of coffee shared with a friend is happiness tasted and time well spent."
Anonymous

Fika Makes Life Taste Better!

Growing up in Sweden, Fika was always the fix when we didn't feel so good — it was as natural as using band aids when we got cut.

Fika is many things

Fika is the combination of coffee, goodies and people wrapped in that sweet feeling of rewarding yourself after a long day and taking a break from the stress and chaos.

Fika is that special oasis where you can sit down for no other purpose than to just enjoy a few moments and be together.

Fika is a time to catch your breath and gain some perspective — a time to share a few laughs, while sipping encouragement and enjoying that irreplaceable feeling of friendship and connection.

Fika is a small, simple thing that anyone can do to create a happier life. Some of us think creating happiness is what life is about — and that is what this book is about!

Why Now?

80 million Americans
report having not even one friend to talk to.

80 million Americans
report being under "extreme stress."

30 million Americans
use some form of antidepressant

The USA is not even in the top 15
happiest countries in the world

According to the World Happiness Report,
the three biggest controllable factors that
determine one's sense of happiness are:

1. Social Connections
2. Health
3. Success at Work.

People Do Not Feel Good!

"The biggest disease today is not leprosy or tuberculosis, but rather the feeling of being unwanted, uncared for, and deserted by everybody."
Mother Teresa

Stress and loneliness are silent killers. Feeling isolated and insignificant creates depression and high levels of stress — and stress is an underlying cause of most illnesses today. It's no coincidence that roughly the same amount of people who report being under "extreme stress" also report having no friends. Loneliness and stress are some of the biggest problems in this country.

"When things go wrong, don't go with them."
Elvis Presley

Stress Makes Us More Lonely
Loneliness Makes Us More Stressed

Loneliness is often regarded as a personal problem, so we feel ashamed about it and keep it quiet. But, when roughly 1/4 of Americans are lonely, it's obvious that it's not only a personal problem. It's a societal problem, and it affects all of us in one way or another.

When we're stressed out, the last thing we want to do is sit down and actually to talk to anybody — we actively avoid it. Instead, we text, email and hide behind our devices, and eventually, we start to avoiding talking to people at all.

When we connect digitally, we get an instant buzz without much effort, quickly followed by an emptiness and hunger for more, and we get addicted. So we keep chasing that next buzz, instead of trying to get the real thing to fulfill that deep-rooted human need for real social connection.

Is the explosion of social media making us less social? We communicate with people on the other side of the world, but we can hardly relate to the people next to us. We are just too busy being busy, hoping to look "successful" in order to live up to the definition of success that we're fed.

"Loneliness has been linked to cognitive decline, so workers who banter with their barista or take coffee breaks together are actually doing a service to their organization." *Phyllis Korkki, New York Times*

"Social isolation is on par with high blood pressure, obesity, lack of exercise, or smoking as a risk factor for illness and early death." *Dr. Cacioppo*

Racing to Death

Many of us hurry through life as if it were a race that we need to win, by reaching the end first. We don't have time to help those falling behind or even stop to take a breath to help ourselves. We don't have time to spend with friends, family and loved ones. We don't have time to invest in our dreams. **We don't have time to have a good time.** We live in a state of time poverty, never feeling we have enough.

"Sleep faster! We need the pillow." *Sign in a Hotel*

We all like to feel good — about ourselves, about life and about the people around us — but, often our desire to feel good is not high on our daily to-do list. There isn't enough time for us to focus on feeling good because we are too busy with the day-to-day things, like work, errands, chores, etc.

Usually, after a long day the need for some good feelings catches up with us, but, by then, we're usually too tired to do much about it. So, we often try to fill that void by searching for instant gratification, like a mouthful of sweets, another episode of our favorite show, or...

"The gratification of desire is not happiness." *Daisaku Ikeda*

"Stress is when you wake up screaming, and
then realize that you haven't fallen asleep yet."
Anonymous

No Time For a Break?

Studies show that, contrary to what we are taught to believe, we get more done if we take breaks. Our brains need breaks to rest up, like athletes need breaks between games. If we work without breaks for hours and hours on end, we get bored, stressed and burned out. If we are constantly stressed, our bodies and minds get no time to recover, so how can we expect them to continue to perform?

"I know what I am trying to escape, but not what I am searching for." *Michel de Montaigne*

Could that be you surfing the web
at work around 3:00?

Productivity skyrockets when the brain feels stimulated, relaxed and engaged. After a break, when you get back at it, you and your brain are open and ready to get new ideas, new perspectives and complete the task much easier and faster.

"Studies show that people who take a break from their work do not do less. It's actually the opposite..." *Professor Vivika Adelsward*

"One of the symptoms of an approaching nervous breakdown is the belief that one's work is terribly important." *Bertrand Russell*

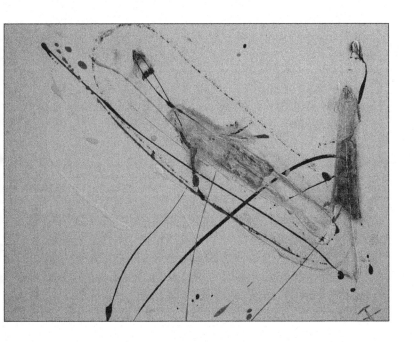

"I'm trying not to put too much pressure on myself, but I think I'm overcompensating. I'm putting too much pressure on myself to not put too much pressure on myself." *Dan Bilardello*

Coffee Breaks Are Good Fika Is Even Better!

Fika is so important to Swedes that it's a fixture in every day's calendar — at home, with friends and even in the workplace. Some of Sweden's biggest companies actually point to Fika as a major ingredient in their formula for success...

> **"More than a coffee break, Fika is a time to share, connect and relax with colleagues. Some of the best ideas and decisions happen at Fika."**
> *Ikea.com*

One of the reasons Fika is so important to Swedish culture and business is that it gives people the opportunity to create and foster relationships that might otherwise fall by the wayside. It's a proven fact that organizations of all kinds — families, companies, societies, etc. — are at their best when their members feel connected to one-another.

"We are social animals, and we have evolved to be in groups. We have always needed others for our survival. It's in our genes." *Professor Tasha R. Howe*

When we are connected to the people around us, we're happy. And, when we're happy, we not only feel better, but we *do* better, too.

Swedes Do It
Several Times Per Day

By supercharging the benefits of breaks with friends, cookies and coffee, Fika addresses many of the major underlying causes of stress and loneliness. It just makes you feel better!

"In all of living, have much fun and laughter. Life is to be enjoyed, not just endured." *Gordon B. Hinckley*

Friends:

More Than Just a Good Time

"Studies indicate that 'social capital' is one of the biggest predictors for health, happiness, and longevity. The problem: we often do not recognize the importance of social connection."
Cecile Andrews, BeWell@Stanford

People who have strong friend groups are happier and healthier than those who don't. On top of that, the number of friends you have is a fairly accurate predictor of how long you will live. Research has actually shown that isolated people are twice as likely to die of heart failure. What good is success if you don't survive to enjoy it?

"Friendship... is not something you learn in school. But if you haven't learned the meaning of friendship, you really haven't learned anything."
Muhammad Ali

"There are no strangers here; only friends you haven't yet met."

William Butler Yeats

Many of us tend to brush friendship aside in times of stress because we don't feel we have time for them when everything else is so hectic. Those moments, though, are actually when it's most important to have a strong support network to keep you going. **Fika combines all the benefits of breaks with the perfect opportunity to build and maintain the friendships we all need!**

"Communication leads to community, that is, to understanding, intimacy and mutual valuing."
Rollo May

Coffee:

Isn't It Bad For You?

**"Our culture runs on coffee and gasoline,
the first often tasting like the second."**
Edward Abbey

Aside from water, coffee is the most common drink
on earth. And, aside from crude oil, it's the biggest
commodity in the world.

Strong Feelings About the Strong Brew

People have consistently loved and hated coffee.
Sometimes it's been sold as a medicine, others it's been
avoided like a poison. People have protested against coffee,
preached of the dangers and maladies it caused, feared it
as the drink of the devil and refused to touch it until the
pope blessed it (which he did).

"Coffee is a language in itself."
Jackie Chan

*In this book, you will learn about the social aspects,
pleasures and values of coffee, and how coffee was used as a
death penalty and reason for divorce, and to win wars and
start revolutions.*

Good News About Coffee

Coffee was once sold as a medicine for all sorts of things, and now research actually shows that it can:

- Lower the risk of diabetes
- Increase metabolism and energy production
- Protect against liver disease
- Protect against parkinson's disease
- Improve thyroid function
- Decrease chance of heart failure
- Lower possibility of dementia and Alzheimer's
- Protect against certain cancers
- Lower risk of death, in general

Plus, a 40-year study showed that people who drink coffee tend to live longer.

"It is inhumane, in my opinion, to force people who have a genuine medical need for coffee to wait in line behind people who apparently view it as some kind of recreational activity." *Dave Barry*

The ABCs of Feeling Good

When we're stressed out, we neither have time nor energy to explore better ways to feel better — and, unfortunately, there are no gyms for working out our happiness muscles! Often, we only learn how to not feel bad, or even feel at all, by escaping into work, TV, internet or different addictions. But what can we actually do to feel better?

"He who has a why to live for can bear any how."
Nietzsche

Fika Fix is our way of sharing our Swedish recipes for coffee, cookies and connection on a smorgosbord of inspiration for living a happier life. Filled with interesting facts, inspiring quotes and simple steps you can take, Fika Fix will show you the ABCs of enjoying the life you deserve, and feeling better right now.

"It is not easy to find happiness in ourselves and it is not possible to find it elsewhere." *Agnes Repplier*

Instead of getting lost in Facebook or clicking through the channels on your TV, try flipping through this book! The ABCs of Feeling Good will show you how to enjoy the life you deserve and feel better right now — one sip at a time.

Varsågod!

"The Constitution only gives people the right to pursue happiness. You have to catch it yourself."
Benjamin Franklin

Attitude

"The greatest discovery of my generation is that a human being can alter his life by altering his attitudes."
William James

Are you controlling your attitude or
is your attitude controlling you?

Just because you wake up in wrinkled pajamas doesn't mean you wear them all day. You can choose to wear something better if you want to look and feel good! It's the same idea with your attitude.

"I, not events, have the power to make me happy or unhappy today. I can choose which one it should be. Yesterday is dead, tomorrow hasn't arrived yet. I have just one day, today, and I'm going to be happy in it."
Groucho Marx

Americano

Equal parts espresso and hot water. It is said that the Americano was first brewed by American GIs in Italy during WWII. The soldiers would dilute espresso with water to make it taste more like the coffee they knew back home, and the Americano was born!

"Attitude is a little thing that makes a big difference." *Winston Churchill*

"Your attitude, not your aptitude, will determine your altitude." Zig Ziglar

Danger!
No Talking Zone

"I fear the day that technology will surpass our human interaction. The world will have a generation of idiots." *Albert Einstein*

The world is becoming faster and louder, but people are becoming more silent.

Instead of living behind the "Do Not Disturb!" sign of a cellphone, computer or headphones when you're around people, why not talk to them?

"Good communication is just as stimulating as black coffee, and just as hard to sleep after."
Anne Morrow Lindbergh

Talking to each other is a very important ingredient in feeling happy. One of the worst punishments is to be put in solitary confinement where you can't talk to anybody. So don't imprison yourself by only hanging out with your computer.

B

Give Yourself A
Break!

"The way we communicate with others and with ourselves ultimately determines the quality of our lives." *Tony Robbins*

If you wanted to make a friend feel good, you would never tell them the things you sometimes tell yourself. *You're so stupid! You look so fat! Nobody likes you!* If you want to make yourself feel better, start treating yourself like a dear friend — and give yourself a break!

"Sometimes I just want someone to hug me and say, 'I know it's hard. You are going to be okay. Here is chocolate and six million dollars." *Anonymous*

Bicerin

Equal parts espresso, drinking chocolate and whole milk. Pour the ingredients into a small, rounded glass, one layer at a time, making sure to keep them separate – that's what makes the drink unique! This drink is a native of Turin, Italy and has been served there since the 18th century.

"Any fool can criticize, condemn and complain. And most fools do." *Benjamin Franklin*

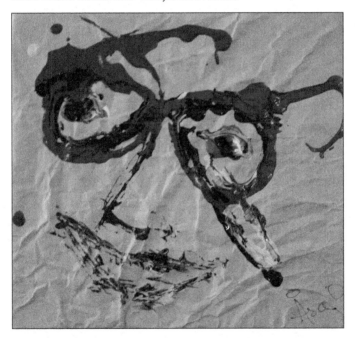

"I speak to everyone in the same way, whether he is the garbage man or the president of the university." *Albert Einstein*

Break it up!

Newton discovered gravity resting under a tree, Archimedes discovered his principle while taking a bath, and Da Vinci took naps all the time! Who says breaks aren't productive?

"Progress isn't made by early risers. It's made by lazy men trying to find easy ways to do something." *Robert Heinlein*

Microbreaks

- Take 5 deep breaths and focus on breathing out
- Run warm water over the insides of your wrists
- Loosen your jaw and gently massage your temples
- Give yourself a quick hand massage
- Stand up and stretch like a yawning cat
- Visualize something that makes you happy
- Smile!

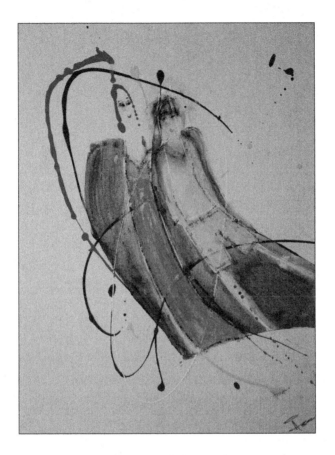

"We will be more successful in all our endeavors if we can let go of the habit of running all the time, and take little pauses to relax and re-center ourselves. And we'll also have a lot more joy in living." *Thich Nhat Hanh*

C

Celebrate!

"Celebrating birthdays promotes health. Statistics show that those who celebrate most birthdays are those who live the longest." *Father Larry Loenezoni*

Our lives may bring a few BIG events like graduations, weddings, promotions, but if we only celebrated those, we would live pretty empty lives. Enjoying the everyday miracles, like a beautiful sunset or having coffee with a friend is an important ingredient in feeling good!

"Fly free and happy beyond birthdays and across forever, and we'll meet now and then when we wish, in the midst of the one celebration that never can end." *Richard David Bach*

Cappuccino

The best cappuccino is made in equal parts: one part espresso, one part steamed milk and one part foamed milk. This drink earned its name because its unique color is very similar to the color of the robes that the Capuchin monks traditionally wear.

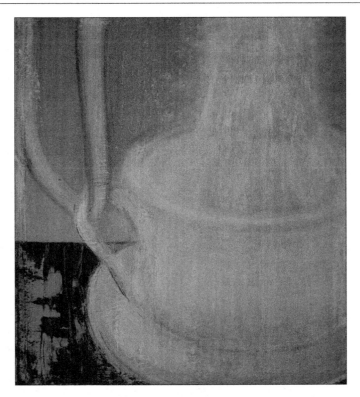

"The more you praise and celebrate your life, the more there is in life to celebrate." *Oprah Winfrey*

Famous Coffee Lovers

"I have tried to show the café as a place where one can go mad." *Vincent Van Gogh*

"Coffee is balm to the heart and spirit."
Verdi

Voltaire is rumored to have drank 50 cups of coffee per day. When someone warned him that it's a slow working poison, he said, **"I believe it. I've been drinking it for 65 years and I'm not dead yet."**

"The powers of a man's mind are directly proportioned to the quantity of coffee he drinks."
Sir James Mcintosh

"Ah! How sweet coffee tastes! Lovelier than a thousand kisses, sweeter far than muscatel wine," Bach wrote in the coffee cantata in 1732.

Like Voltaire, Honoré de Balzac is also rumored to have drank nearly 50 cups of coffee per day, but Balzac mixed it with bourbon, martinique and mocha and then boiled it to a strong syrupy brew. It's said that sometimes he would even chew the beans raw, just to get the caffeine.

D

Dare To Do It!

"All worthwhile men have good thoughts, good ideas and good intentions - but precious few of them ever translate those into action." *John Hancock*

Sometimes we let other people — and ourselves — stop us from doing what we really want to do. Daring to take the first little step toward creating the life you want and having the courage to meet new people and do new things is the foundation for creating a happy, successful life.

"I'd rather regret the things I've done than regret the things I haven't done." *Lucille Ball*

Down-Under Iced Coffee

One cup of chilled coffee, one scoop of ice cream, maple syrup to taste, topped with whipped cream and chocolate shavings. A classic Australian take on the regular ol' iced coffee.

"We can't do everything at once, but we can do something at once." *Calvin Coolidge*

Almost 2/3 of Americans Don't Get Any Recognition at Work

"One of the most important things you can do on this earth is to let people know they are not alone." *Shannon L. Alder*

Dare to Make Someone's Day!

"When we feel love and kindness toward others, it not only makes others feel loved and cared for, but it helps us also to develop inner happiness and peace." *Dalai Lama*

Try this! Next time you're buying a coffee, buy a "suspended coffee" for somebody else down the line. At some places, everybody pays for somebody else's coffee, not their own. Pay it forward!

"I don't know what your destiny will be, but one thing I do know: the only ones among you who will be really happy are those who have sought and found how to serve." *Albert Schweitzer*

Express Enthusiasm

"If you have zest and enthusiasm you attract zest and enthusiasm. Life does give back in kind."
Norman Vincent Peale

We are magnets, and we attract what we focus on. So, if you want to feel good, focus on the good in yourself and others.

Enthusiasm is so contagious! So why not be someone you would want to be around, yourself? You just might find that other people want to be around you, too!

"Positive thinking is more than just a tagline. It changes the way we behave. And I firmly believe that when I am positive, it not only makes me better, but it also makes those around me better." *Harvey Mackay*

Espresso

Espresso (not eXpresso) is strong coffee that is made by forcing steam through finely ground, roasted coffee beans — surprisingly enough, the same beans you find in regular coffee. A good shot of Espresso will have a layer of golden-brown crema on top. One Espresso shot has 1/3 of the caffeine of a regular cup of coffee.

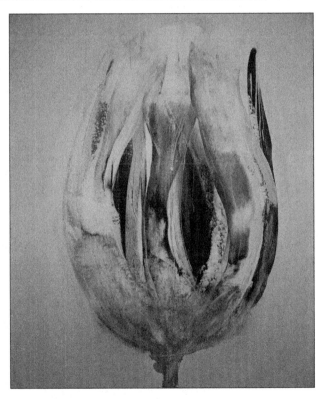

"Choosing the freedom to be uninteresting never quite worked for me." *Diane Keaton*

For the Love of Coffee

"Almost all my middle aged and elderly acquaintances, including me, feel about 25, unless we haven't had our coffee, in which case we feel 107." *Martha Beck*

In old Constantinople, women weren't allowed inside the coffee houses, but coffee was so important to the culture that a husband's failure to provide his wife with coffee at home was grounds for divorce.

"Life without coffee is like love without kisses." *Swedish Saying*

"Behind every successful man is a surprised woman." *Maryon Pearson*

"Behind every successful woman is a substantial amount of coffee." *Stephanie Piro*

Focus on Feeling Good!

"The big thing is not what happens to us in life, but what we do about what happens to us."
George H. Allen

Life presents us with so many negative images and situations that it takes a conscious effort to shift our focus to things that actually bring us happiness. It's like that old self-fulfilling prophecy: when you buy a yellow car, you suddenly see them everywhere. When you focus on feeling good, you find and create reasons to feel good everywhere.

"You can't prevent birds of sorrow from flying over your head. But you can prevent them from building a nest in your hair." *Chinese Proverb*

Flat White

Two shots Espresso topped with microfoam. The difference between this and a cappuccino is that the flat white uses micro-foam (uniformly 'gooey' steamed milk with tiny bubbles) and the cappuccino uses dry foam ('foamy' milk with large bubbles). The Flat White is ideal for creating latte art.

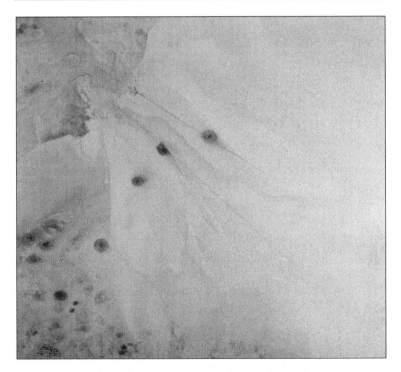

"If we only wanted to be happy, it would be easy; but we want to be happier than other people, and that is almost always difficult, since we think them happier than they are." *Charles de Montesquieu*

Fika Fitness!

Tips for making Fika feel better for you and everyone else!

It's always a good idea to treat those around you how you would like them to treat you and others.

"Everyone thinks of changing the world, but no one thinks of changing himself."
Leo Tolstoy

Disinfect Yourself

From negativity, complaints and criticism.

"Correction does much, but encouragement does more." *Goethe*

Make it Special

Create a nice setting to share a tasty treat.

"My mom's funny that way, celebrating special occasions with blue food. I think it's her way of saying anything is possible. Percy can pass seventh grade. Waffles can be blue. Little miracles like that." *Rick Riordan*

Listen up!

"Most of the successful people I've known are the ones who do more listening than talking." *Bernard M. Baruch*

Paying attention, rather than just looking for your turn to speak or letting your mind wander is a crucial ingredient for keeping yourself engaged with a Fika partner.

"It's a rare person who wants to hear what he doesn't want to hear." *Dick Cavett*

"It's better to be absolutely ridiculous than absolutely boring." *Marilyn Monroe*

G

Be Grateful!

"There's always something to be thankful for. If you can't pay your bills, you can be thankful you're not one of your creditors." *Anonymous*

A growing field of science is showing that one of the greatest contributing factors to overall happiness in life is how much gratitude you show. Many experts say that shifting a habitual negative mindset to one of gratitude and appreciation will lead to better sleep, improved health and boosted energy.

"As we express our gratitude, we must never forget that the highest appreciation is not to utter words, but to live by them." *John F. Kennedy*

Galão

One part Espresso, three parts hot milk and sugar to taste. For maximum fanciness, serve this Portuguese staple in a tall glass.

"Good men and bad men differ radically. Bad men never appreciate kindness shown them, but wise men appreciate and are grateful. Wise men try to express their appreciation and gratitude by some return of kindness, not only to their benefactor, but to everyone."
Buddha

Keep a Journal
To Feel Better

**Research has shown that
Journaling can lead to:**
- *Boosted IQ*
- *Better Memory*
- *Expanded Creativity*
- *Improved Problem Solving*
- *Increased Mental Clarity*
- *Reduced Levels of Stress*
- *Higher Chances of reaching goals*

It's easy! Even five minutes of journaling per day can deliver these benefits. To see the quickest results, try to end your journaling with at least five successes from that day and five things you are grateful for, even little things like clean air to breathe.

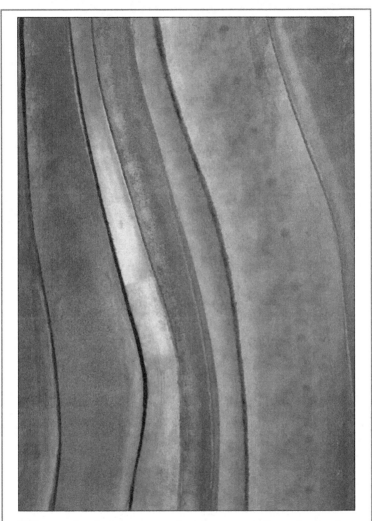

"Happy is the person who does not show hatred
over what is gone, but instead shows gratefulness
for what is left." *Anonymous*

Health

"Physical fitness is not only one of the most important keys to a healthy body, it is the basis of dynamic and creative intellectual activity."
John F. Kennedy

Take Care of Your Body!
It Should Last a Lifetime

If you're feeling down, a little bit of exercise helps shake off bad moods and extra pounds. Many of the most successful people in the world point to exercise as one of their most important habits because it gives more energy than it takes, and studies have even shown that exercise is sometimes more effective than antidepressants at treating depression. Also, many experts agree that fitness begins in the kitchen.

"Being fit and healthy, there's nothing like the endorphins from being fit, and the incredible endorphin rush that goes with that." *Richard Branson*

Hot Coffee Masala

One cup of coffee, ½ cup milk, two cumin seeds, one whole star anise pod, one tsp cinnamon and two tsp sugar. In scalding hot coffee, mix in all ingredients except milk. Remove seeds and pod after 3-4 minutes. Add hot milk.

"When is the best time to start exercising? About 15 years ago." *Anonymous*

Death by Coffee?

Gustav III, the king of Sweden in the late 1700s, was very suspicious of coffee. In an attempt to scare people away from the drink and the conversations it could lead to, he thought up a cruel experiment:

To prove the deadly effects of the foul substance, twins convicted of murder were sentenced to death by coffee. One twin was forced to drink 3 pots of coffee per day and the other, 3 pots of tea. Gustav's plan was to show how quickly the coffee would kill the first twin as compared to his identical tea-drinking brother. Gustav ordered two doctors to oversee the experiment and tell him as soon as one of the twins died.

Unfortunately for Gustav III, before either of the twins succumbed to their punishment, he was murdered and both doctors died. Finally, at the ripe old age of 83 years old, the first of the twins died... and, ironically enough, it was the tea-drinker.

"The irony is, the more you try to control life
and others, the more out of control you feel."
Adyashanti

I

Intention

A clear intention is the secret ingredient for success in achieving even our smallest goals with ease, instead of stressing through the day and pushing to complete what we have to.

If you want to feel better, set a clear intention of easily getting things done while having fun, instead of just dreading another day at work or another chore.

Indian Filter Coffee

Add 2 of tablespoons of chicory to the grinds you would use in a regular drip maker. This is a simplified version of the Indian tradition of brewing this beverage, but the original involves several unique brewing pieces and an amazing display of pouring the coffee back and forth from one container to the other, which earned the beverage the nickname "meter coffee."

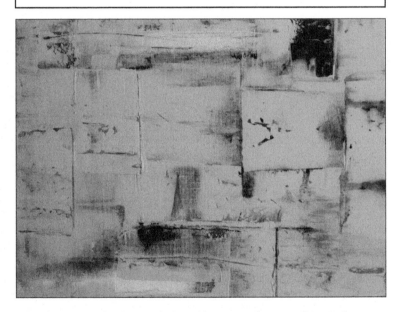

Passion is a feeling that tells you: this is the right thing to do. Nothing can stand in my way. It doesn't matter what anyone else says. This feeling is so good that it cannot be ignored. I'm going to follow my bliss and act upon this glorious sensation of joy."
Wayne W. Dyer

Busy Being Busy?

Many of us are so busy just being busy because we're constantly interrupted by little things like texts or emails, and we don't have time to do the things that actually make us feel good.. Studies show that small interruptions steal more time than you think. They actually offset your workflow by several minutes beyond what it takes to actually read the text or check your Facebook.

"75% of my life is spent wasting time. The other 25% isn't nearly as productive." *Jarod Kintz*

Try This! Make time for the things you like! Commit to 50 minutes of uninterrupted work, followed by 10 minutes of checking on all the "other" stuff. It can really help you get much more done!

"A man who dares to waste one hour of time has not discovered the value of life." *Charles Darwin*

J

Just Joke!

"Life is worth living as long as there's a laugh in it."
L.M. Montgomery

Humor is often the first thing to go when we get stressed and busy. Try to find any excuse to laugh, like funny videos, jokes, a mirror… etc. When you read or watch uplifting or funny things, your immune system, mood and general sense of wellbeing improve. If you're looking for the one magic ingredient to feeling good, it has to be humor.

"After God created the world, He made man and woman. Then, to keep the whole thing from collapsing, He invented humor." *Guillermo Mordillo*

Jamocha

Two cups of coffee, one cup of milk, two cups of vanilla ice cream, one dash of salt, one dash of sugar and chocolate syrup to taste. Blend all ingredients together until smooth. Coffee, ice cream, chocolate and a hilarious name... what's not to love?

"Don't laugh at coffee, someday you, too, may be old and weak." *Anonymous*

"One loses many laughs by not laughing at oneself."
Sara Jeanette Duncan

Laugh More!

Research shows that we laugh a lot less now than just 30 years ago, and the negative impact that has on our happiness, health and stress levels is immense.

"God writes a lot of comedy... the trouble is, he's stuck with so many bad actors who don't know how to play funny." *Garrison Keillor*

"You grow up the day you have your first real laugh at yourself." *Ethyl Barrymore*

but

"It's hard to enjoy practical jokes when your whole life feels like one." *Rick Riordan*

Just remember, if it will be funny to tell someone in a few years — it is funny now!

"Comedy is tragedy plus time." *Carol Brunette*

When we look at life through the lens of humor we start to see the world differently...

"From there to here, from here to there, funny things are everywhere!" *Dr. Seuss*

Too Much?
"Opera is when a guy gets stabbed in the back and, instead of bleeding, he sings." *Robert Benchley*

Too Late?
"I never drink coffee at lunch. I find it keeps me awake for the afternoon." *Ronald Reagan*

Too Hot?
"Go to heaven for the climate and hell for the company." *Benjamin Franklin Wade*

Too Hungry?
"Ask not what you can do for your country. Ask what's for lunch." *Orson Welles*

Too True?
"In politics, stupidity is not a handicap."
Napoléon Bonaparte

Too Distracting?
"A girl in a bikini is like having a loaded pistol on your coffee table — There's nothing wrong with them, but it's hard to stop thinking about it." *Garrison Keillor*

Too Weak?
"If this is coffee, then please bring me some tea. If this is tea, please bring me some coffee."*Abraham Lincoln*

K

Kindness

"You cannot do a kindness too soon, for you never know how soon it will be too late." *Ralph Waldo Emerson*

Finally, science is able to prove what many of us already know: how being kind is actually very selfish. Random, little acts of kindness — like buying the person behind you a cup of coffee — make every single person involved feel better. And it's easy! You don't even have to do anything big to get this effect. In fact, little, consistent acts of kindness have been shown to be the most rewarding.

"Unexpected kindness is the most powerful, least costly and most underrated agent of human change." *Bob Kerrey*

Kopi Luwak

Chances are you will never get to try this coffee and you may not want to! It's some of the most expensive coffee in the world, sometimes priced at $1500 per lb and it comes from the digestive tract of an Asian palm civet (cat-like creature.) They eat the coffee berry and poop out the bean, supposedly tastier than it went in.

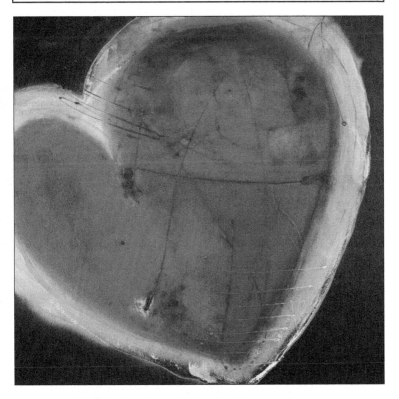

"Noble deeds and hot baths are the best cures for depression." *Dudey Smith*

Be a Kind Mirror

"It is an absolute human certainty that no one can know his own beauty of perceive a sense of his own worth until it has been reflected back to him in the mirror of another, loving, caring human being." *John Joseph Powell*

When we get caught up in the daily "busyness," we often get very self-centered, and start to look at other people as competitors or distractions, rather than potential friends or allies. Try to look for ways to make others feel better, and you will almost certainly feel better, too.

"Giving is the secret of a healthy life. Not necessarily money, but whatever a man has of encouragement, sympathy and understanding." *John D. Rockefeller Jr.*

"It is literally true, that you can succeed best and quickest by helping others to succeed." *Napoleon Hill*

"A person who is nice to you, but rude to the waiter, is not a nice person." *Dave Barry*

L

Let it Go!

"Some of us think holding on makes us strong; but sometimes it is letting go." *Hermann Hesse*

No matter how well you cook an old, spoiled piece of meat, it's never going to taste good. Don't expect your life to taste good, either, if you hold onto old, spoiled habits, memories and grudges.

"Never look back unless you are planning to go that way." *Henry David Thoreau*

Latte

One part espresso, two parts steamed milk, add layer of foamed milk to top. The Latte as we know it is an American creation, claimed by a coffee shop owner in Berkeley, CA. In Italian, "latte" literally means milk, so ordering a latte in Italy will probably get you what you ordered: a glass of milk.

"Holding a grudge is like drinking poison and waiting for the other person to die." *William Shakespeare*

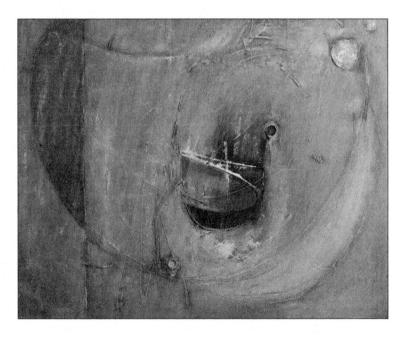

"Forgiveness is setting someone else free and then realizing that you were the prisoner." *Max Lucado*

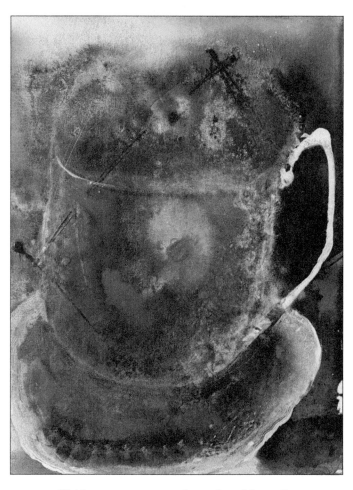

"Life moves on and so should we."
Spencer Johnson

18 Unexpectedly Awesome Uses for Coffee Grounds

- Repel Slugs and Other Pests
- Fertilize Your Garden
- Turbocharge Your Compost
- Naturally Cleanse Your Hair
- Exfoliate Your Skin
- Clean Out the Fireplace
- Treat Your Cellulite
- Fuel Your Worms
- Absorb Food Odors
- Deter Cats
- Scour Your Pans
- Clean and Deodorize Your Drains
- Tenderize Your Meat
- Make an Air Freshener
- Remove Dark Circles from Under Your Eyes
- Clean a Dirty Grill
- Clean Your Hands
- Erase Scratches From Your Furniture

"I like the serendipitous surprises of reality."
Lawrence Wright

M

Music

"I know music makes chickens lay more eggs and factory workers produce more. But how much more can they get out of an elevator?"
Victor Borge

————————

Music has an enormous impact on our feelings. Imagine a sad scene in a movie with happy music in the background. It would be comical! So score your life with some happy music and feel better!

————————

"When she started to play, Steinway came down personally and rubbed his name off the piano."
Bob Hope

"Wagner's music is better than it sounds."
Mark Twain

Mocha

Add a shot of Espresso to your favorite hot chocolate.
Coffee + chocolate = Mocha.

"Coffee and chocolate — the inventor of mocha should be sainted." *Cherise Sinclair*

"He who hears music, feels his solitude peopled at once."
Robert Browning

Coffee House Inspiration

"I don't know where my ideas come from. I will admit, however, that one key ingredient is caffeine. I get a couple cups of coffee into me and weird things just start to happen." *Gary Larson*

Research shows that a moderate level of distraction — like the sounds of a coffee house — can actually boost your creativity and productivity. If you can't make it to a coffee house, you can get the sound of coffee houses right on your phone; there are videos on youtube, apps and entire websites dedicated to giving you the feeling of being in a coffee house.

"Inspiration is the greatest gift because it opens your life to many new possibilities. Each day becomes more meaningful, and your life is enhanced when your actions are guided by what inspires you." *Bernie Siegel*

"Way too much coffee. But if it weren't for the coffee, I'd have no identifiable personality whatsoever." *David Letterman*

N

New Lifestyle

"When you're finished changing, you're finished."
Benjamin Franklin

Doing new things can be a quick way to pick yourself up from a slump. If you're feeling down, instead of retreating into your comfort zone, push your boundaries and try something new. Studies have shown that we feel very tired when we are bored, but doing new things can energize and excite us. Some say we stop being curious when we get older... Or is it that we grow old when we stop being curious?

"Your life does not get better by chance, it gets better by change." *Jim Rohn*

Naked Cappuccino

One shot espresso, one shot hot water, foam. Basically an Americano with foam... A stripped version of the cappuccino!

"I have no special talents. I am only passionately curious." *Albert Einstein*

"Change is not a four letter word, but often your reaction to it is." *Jeffrey Gitomer*

Coffee in a Sock

"The difficulty lies not so much in developing new ideas as in escaping from old ones."
John Maynard Keynes

Melitta Coffee Filter

Until the early 1900s, coffee filters were made of cloth, and sometimes people would even use clothing. One day, Melitta Bentz decided she was tired of using socks to make her coffee, so she used a piece of paper from her son's homework, and changed the coffee-brewing process forever.

"To invent, you need a good imagination and a pile of junk." *Thomas A. Edison*

"You don't learn to walk by following rules. You learn by doing and by falling over." *Richard Branson*

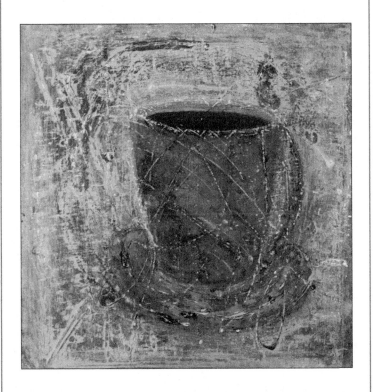

"I have not failed. I have just found **10,000** ways that won't work." *Thomas Edison*

O

Optimism

"Positive thinking is more than just a tagline. It changes the way we behave. And I firmly believe that when I am positive, it not only makes me better, but it also makes those around me better." *Harvey Mackay*

One of the main ingredients in feeling good is optimism! It's not some foofy thing, it's actually a proven technique for creating a happier, wealthier and healthier life. Looking at challenges like a body builder looks at heavier weights is a great approach to becoming optimistic.

"The way I see it, if you want the rainbow, you've gotta put up with the rain." *Dolly Parton*

Organic Coffee

Organic coffee is grown without the use of chemical fertilizers and pesticides, and therefore maintains the natural nutrients of the coffee bean . Organic coffee is healthier and better for the environment than the standard bean. And if it's fair trade, it is better for the people, too. Look into it!

"I am an optimist. It does not seem much use being anything else." *Winston Churchill*

"Happiness is not the absence of problems, it's the ability to deal with them." *Steve Maraboli*

Be Lucky!

"I'm a great believer in luck and I find the harder I work the more I have of it." *Thomas Jefferson*

Research shows that only 10 percent of luck is determined by chance. The other 90 percent is in your own hands. You create your own luck!

"Luck is not a magical ability or a gift from the gods... Instead, it is a way of thinking and behaving." *Richard Wiseman*

The luckiest people are those who have mastered the art of turning any situation into a good one. So, by working to make yourself feel good, you also make yourself more lucky, which will probably make you feel even better!

"Success is simply a matter of luck. Ask any failure." *Earl Wilson*

"Shallow men believe in luck or in circumstance. Strong men believe in cause and effect." *Ralph Waldo Emerson*

P

Patience

What do we want? **Patience!**
When do we want it? **Now!**

Part of making a cake is letting it have time to bake in the oven. You just can't rush it by cranking up the heat. Often it's the same way with creating good things in life. It takes time, and that's okay!

"I couldn't wait for success, so I went ahead without it." *Jonathan Winters*

Palazzo

Two shots of iced espresso, mixed with sweet cream to taste. This drink is very popular in southern California and is traditionally made using a moka pot.

"Time is our most valuable asset, yet we tend to waste it, kill it and spend it rather than invest it." *Jim Rohn*

"You can have it all. Just not all at once."
Oprah Winfrey

Be Present
in the Present

"The people who get most out of life are not those who lived for a century, but those who lived every minute." *Collette*

It's easy to get stressed when you are caught up in the drama of the future or past, and forget to experience what is in front of you right now. Sometimes, taking a minute to clear your mind and take a few deep breaths can help you come back to where you are right now.

"And in the end, it's not the years in your life that count. It's the life in your years." *Abraham Lincoln*

"Mindfulness is often spoken of as the heart of Buddhist meditation. It's not about Buddhism, but about paying attention. That's what all meditation is, no matter what tradition or particular technique is used." *Jon Kabat-Zinn*

Q

Quiet Your Mind

"It takes courage to endure the sharp pains of self-discovery, rather than choose to take the dull pain of unconsciousness that would last the rest of our lives." Marianne Williamson

---

Creating quiet time for oneself is one of the best ways to reduce stress and enhance wellbeing, and it's something most successful people have in common. Whether it's taking a quiet walk on the beach, a yoga class or even just sitting by yourself for a few minutes, the key is to create some quiet time in the middle of even the craziest week.

"There are three things extremely hard: steel, a diamond, and to know oneself." Benjamin Franklin

Queen's Cup

Two shots of espresso, one scoop of vanilla ice cream. Drizzle with syrup of your choice and serve in the fanciest cup available — no mugs allowed! Pinkies up.

"There were some problems only coffee and ice cream could fix." *Amal El-Mohtar*

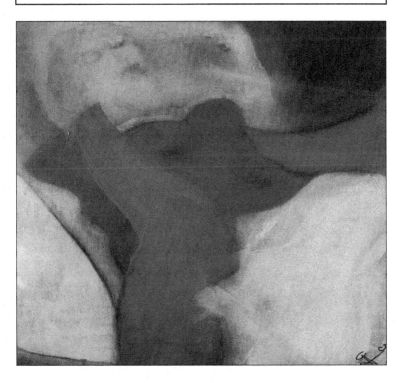

"It takes a lot of time to be a genius. You have to sit around so much, doing nothing, really doing nothing." *Gertrude Stein*

Listen In!

"As soon as you trust yourself, you will know how to live." *Goethe*

Practice listening to and trusting yourself. Of course, your own ideas will not always be perfect, but there's usually a reason why you think or feel a certain way instead of another. Listen to it and learn from it. Nobody knows you better than you do.

"Men do not trust themselves anymore, and when that happens there is nothing left except perhaps to find some strong sure man, even though he may be wrong, and to dangle from his coattails." *John Steinbeck*

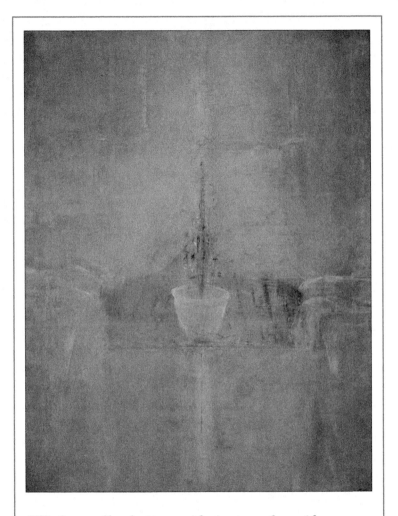

"We have all a better guide in ourselves, if we
would attend to it, than any other person can be."
Jane Austen

R

Roll With It!

"Stay committed to your decisions, but stay flexible in your approach." *Tony Robbins*

Many of us have a desire to control and organize everything that happens in our lives. But, at a certain point, being flexible and willing to accept what may be beyond our control can not only help us focus on what we can control, but also feel better knowing we are not responsible for the entire world.

"I am a man of fixed and unbending principles, the first of which is to be flexible at all times." *Everett Dirksen*

Red Eye

One cup coffee, one (or two or three) shots of espresso. It's basically coffee with more coffee... This is guaranteed to keep your red eyes wide open after taking the red eye flight. This drink is sometimes called a "shot in the dark."

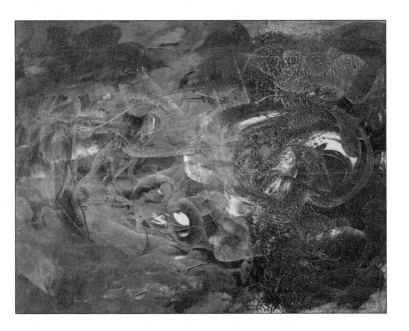

"You must be shapeless, formless, like water. When you pour water in a cup, it becomes the cup. When you pour water in a bottle, it becomes the bottle. When you pour water in a teapot, it becomes the teapot. Water can drip and it can crash. Become like water my friend." *Bruce Lee*

Make Coffee, Not War

As soon as the Civil War broke out, the Union cut off the Confederacy's access to coffee, and the Confederacy cut off the Union's access to Tobacco. During brief moments of peace, opposing soldiers would meet in the fields and exchange the two.

> **"We are reduced to quarter rations and no coffee... And nobody can soldier without coffee."**
> *Ebenezer Nelson Gilpin*

The word "coffee" was more present in the diaries of the Civil War soldiers than almost any other word... including "war," "slavery," "mother," and even "Lincoln."

> **"If your men get their coffee early in the morning, you can hold."** *Gen. Benjamin Butler*

Coffee played such a big role in the war, that Sharps Rifle Co. began making a rifle with a grinder built into the handle.

During WWII, Sweden's access to coffee was cut off. In desperation, the Swedes developed 144 coffee substitutes... None of them did the trick.

S

Smile!

A smile is more infectious than the common cold and, instead of getting everybody sick for two weeks, your smile can actually make everybody else feel better. If we see someone smiling, we instinctively smile back. And, even if you're all alone, a smile can be a great pick-me-up. One of the easiest, most surprising shortcuts to happiness and success is smiling.

"Practice smiling. Smile at lampposts and mailboxes. Don't be modest — this isn't the time." *Jacque Mercer*

Short Black

Double shot of espresso served in a glass.

"I think, if I were a woman, I'd wear coffee as a perfume." *John VanDruten*

The Amazing Effects of a
Simple Smile

- Boost your mood
- Destress
- Lower your heart rate
- Increase your productivity
- Boost perceived trustworthiness
- Reduce your pain
- Increase attractiveness
- Reduce perceived age
- Boost immune system
- Increase chances of success

"I'm really exciting. I smile a lot, I win a lot, and I'm really sexy."
Serena Williams

HAVE A SMILE!

"Can you hear me smiling?"
My 3 year old on the phone.

"Happiness is the only good. The time to be happy is now. The place to be happy is here.
The way to be happy is to make others so."

"Taking joy in life is a woman's best cosmetic." Rosalind Russell

"Practice smiling. Smile at lamp posts and mail boxes. don't be modest- this isn't the time. Always eat a snack before going to a luncheon meeting so you can spend your time charming and not chewing." Jacque Mercer (Former miss America on how to win a beauty contest.)

HAVE ONE -THEY ARE FREE!
(and share it!)

"A smile is the light in your window that tells others that there is a caring, sharing person inside."
Denis Waitley

95

Touch

"Too often we underestimate the power of a touch, a smile, a kind word, a listening ear, an honest compliment or the smallest act of caring, all of which have the potential to turn a life around." *Leo Buscaglia*

Touch is essential for our wellbeing, and also a time-tested mood-booster. Often, we are too busy to really hug the people we care about and we miss out on all the free endorphines and happiness horomones that come with simple touching. We say, *keep in touch, that was a touching story* and *you touched my heart* because on a certain level we all know how important touch is.

"Touch is a more powerful communicator than words." *Marty Rubin*

Turkish Coffee

*Grind your beans extra fine. Place 1.5 tbsp of ground coffee, a small pinch of cardamom and another of cinnamon, and sugar to taste into one cup of water and heat over medium heat. Do not stir yet. When you see the mix is on the verge of boiling, turn the heat to low. Begin to stir the brew with a spoon or whisk to build the signature 'foam' of Turkish Coffee. If it starts to boil, remove from heat for a few moments to cool down and repeat process. Pour into fancy cups and enjoy! *Do not drink grinds at bottom — let settle for one minute before drinking.*

"Coffee should be black as hell, strong as death and sweet as love." *Turkish Proverb*

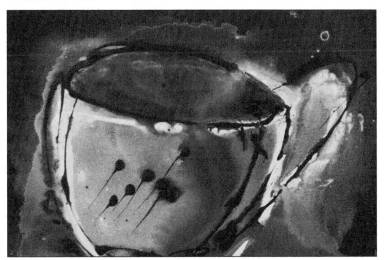

"Sometimes, reaching out and taking someone's hand is the beginning of a journey. At other times, it is allowing another to take yours." *Vera Nazarian*

A Touchy Subject!

"Coffee leads men to trifle away their time, scald their chops, and spend their money, all for a little base, black, thick, nasty, bitter, stinking, nauseous puddle of water."

1674, London. Women formed a group to protest that their men were always at the coffee houses, and not at home as needed during domestic crises. Thus, the Women's Petition Against Coffee was born...

U
Unleash
Your Inner Viking!

"It is not death that man should fear, but he should fear never beginning to live." *Marcus Aurelius*

To unleash your Inner Viking means having the courage to step up when you're facing challenges or uncertainty, and taking the risk to let go of the comfort of the familiar and explore new possibilities. Unleashing your Inner Viking means having the strength and character to live a fearless life and stand up for what you think is right. There's just no substitute for integrity and courage when it comes to geeling good about yourself.

"In life, finding a voice is speaking and living the truth. Each of you is an original. Each of you, has a distinctive voice. When you find it, your story will be told. You will be heard." *John Grisham*

Unfiltered Coffee

*A very simple way to make a good, strong cuppa. Place four tsp finely ground coffee per cup of water into a pot. Bring to a boil. Pour into a cup and drink. *Do not drink grinds — let settle one minute before drinking.*

"For the past 33 years, I have looked in the mirror every morning and asked myself: "If today were the last day of my life, would I want to do what I am about to do today?" And whenever the answer has been "no" for too many days in a row, I know I need to change something." *Steve Jobs*

Management by Fika

Fika is one of the Swedes' biggest secrets to not only success, but general employee wellbeing and loyalty. Many bosses say the 30 minutes spent on Fika are some of the best and most effective they spend all day.

"...It's important to listen to everyone and through the communal nature of Fika, chatting between employees and management is encouraged. It's a great way to get everyone's view on how companies are run." *Andreas Åström, Stockholm Chamber of Commerce*

"'Police work wouldn't be possible without coffee,' Wallander said.
'No work would be possible without coffee.'
They pondered the importance of coffee in silence." *Henning Mankell, Bestselling Swedish Author*

"Swedes are the masters of informal networking – they even invented a word for meeting up and talking over a cup of coffee: to "Fika." It's both a verb and a noun. Most of all, it's an incredible way to meet new people and exchange ideas." *Marco Ortolani, program director of Berghs Certificate*

"Do Lipton employees take coffee breaks?"
Steven Wright

V

Visualize

"To accomplish great things we must first dream, then visualize, then plan... believe... act!" *Alfred A. Montapert*

Feeling good takes practice, like anything else you want to be good at. Visualization is an easy, effective way to practice feeling good. By creating a clear, specific vision of what you want and enthusiastically feeling it as if it has already taken place, you actually help to create it faster.

"You must give everything to make your life as beautiful as the dreams that dance in your imagination." *Roman Payne*

Vienna

Two shots espresso, ½ tbsp sugar, ½ tsp vanilla extract and ice.
Blend ingredients until smooth. Serve in a fancy glass and add
one scoop ice cream and a dusting of unsweetened cocoa powder.

**"The harder you work... and visualize something, the
luckier you get."** *Seal*

Schools of Wisdom

In Constantinople, coffeehouses were so highly regarded that they were called "Qahveh Khaneh," which means "Schools of Wisdom."

From Medicine to Fuel for Revolution

Coffee was once seen mainly as medicine, but between the 16th and 18th centuries, coffee's popularity skyrocketed all across Europe. By the mid 18th century, there were over 600 coffee houses in Paris alone.

Along with the rise of coffee houses came the rise of the age of reason and, with that, the age of rebellion. All of a sudden, people could have intelligent and meaningful conversations in public, without the numbing effects of alcohol. And this meant kings suddenly had to be concerned about the conversations that were taking place in coffee houses, as those could easily lead to rebellion… Which they often did.

"No one can understand the truth until he drinks
a coffee's frothy goodness." *Sheikh Abd-Al-Kadir*

Wow Factor!

"The difference between ordinary and extraordinary is that little extra." *Jimmy Johnson*

The wow factor is that extra something that gives color to your life, that makes you feel enthusiastic, energized and passionate. Many people think money is the default wow factor, but beyond the level needed for survival and comfort, money has been proven to have little influence on happiness and fulfillment. So what could yours be? *What gets you excited? What you would do if money were no question? What do you feel strongly about?* Try to create at least one "Wow!" every day. *"Wow! What a beautiful morning!"*

"If you love your work, you'll be out there every day trying to do it the best you possibly can, and pretty soon everybody around will catch the passion from you — like a fever." *Sam Walton*

White Chocolate Latte

One cup milk, one tsp heavy cream, one tsp sugar. Combine ingredients in sauce pan. Heat and stir until hot and frothy. Pour into mug with two shots of espresso, a handful of white chocolate chips (to taste) and a dash of vanilla extract.

"If a man is called to be a street sweeper, he should sweep streets even as a Michaelangelo painted, or Beethoven composed music or Shakespeare wrote poetry. He should sweep streets so well that all the hosts of heaven and earth will pause to say, 'Here lived a great street sweeper who did his job well.'" *Martin Luther King Jr.*

Shared Joy is Double Joy
Shared Sorrow is Half Sorrow.
Swedish Proverb

When you feel empathy and oneness with other people, their wins and joy become yours, too. Sharing coffee or breaking bread with someone is an ancient tradition of bonding – it's basically in our genes

---

"When you start to develop your powers of empathy and imagination, the whole world opens up to you." *Susan Sarandon*

"The great gift of human beings is
that we have the power of empathy."
Meryl Streep

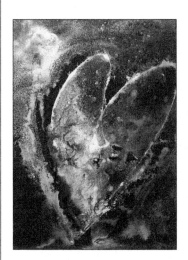 

"Empathy is about finding echoes
of another person in yourself."
Mohsin Hamid

Xperiment

"All life is an experiment. The more experiments you make the better." *Ralph Waldo Emerson*

Sometimes, we hold ourselves back because we are afraid of making mistakes and taking risks. Mistakes are your stepping stones to excellence! Don't be afraid to try new things. If you always order a cappuccino, try tea. Allow your tastes to change as you change — you just might find your new favorite thing where you never thought you would. Xperimenting helps you find and refine your own taste, so you don't end up stuck in a rut.

"The greatest mistake you can make in life is to be continually fearing you will make one." *Elbert Hubbard*

Xtra strong coffee!

Add a scoop of collagen or protein powder to your morning coffee to get an xtra good, supercharged start to your day!

"Have no fear of perfection, you will never reach it."
Salvador Dali

"There's no secret about success. Did you ever know a successful man who didn't tell you about it?" *Kin Hubbard*

Listen and Learn!

"Learn from the mistakes of others, you can't live long enough to make them all yourself." *Anonymous*

Most successful leaders list being a good listener as one of their top strengths. One of the many, many reasons is that learning from those around you can save you a lot of time, frustration and energy.

"I didn't list listening as one of my skills, probably because I didn't hear what the interviewer asked." *Jarod Kintz*

Yes!

Saying "Yes!" to uncertainty is important. Clinging to familiarity or sticking with what you know may work for a while, but if you want to go further it's important to say "Yes!" to the unknown to find something that works even better. Part of success is helping others be successful, too. So, when a friend really needs your support, try to say "Yes!"

Yuang Yuang

One cup coffee, ½ can sweetened condensed milk, two black tea bags, ½ cup water. Heat water to a gentle boil, add tea bags for three minutes, remove tea and add condensed milk. Heat and stir for three minutes and add to coffee.

"You miss 100 percent of the shots you don't take."
Wayne Gretzky

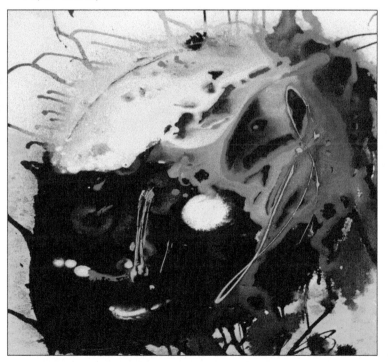

"There are an infinite number of reasons to say no. Instead, try to focus on one good reason to say yes."
Jarod Kintz

Fika Flirtation

"Gravitation is not responsible for people falling in love." *Albert Einstein*

Well, if it's not gravity, maybe it's Fika...

_____

Fika is the most popular option for a first date in Sweden, and it makes sense! It's a non-pretentious, friendly way to get to know somebody.

"I was nauseous and tingly all over. I was either in love or I had smallpox." *Woody Allen*

Fika is is also the perfect way to nurture love that has been tested by time. Fika gives us the opportunity to put the spark back into those relationships that are so easy to take for granted.

_____

"Before you marry a person, you should first make them use a computer with slow Internet service to see who they really are." *Will Ferrell*

"In this world, it is too common for people to search for someone to lose themselves in. But I am already lost. I will look for someone to find myself in." *C. Joybell C.*

ZZZleep

It's hard to feel good — or be good at anything — when you're exhausted, so make sleep a priority! But it's not only about the quantity of sleep, the quality of your sleep plays a very important role, too. Too much stress can ruin a good night's sleep, so try to destress as much as possible before bed. Just remember stress can come from inside, or from watching depressing news and violent TV shows.

Zestpresso

Grind a little bit of cinnamon, nutmeg and cloves into your coffee grinds before brewing. Or if you buy pre-ground, just add the spices into the mixture. Start out LIGHT with the spices and add more if you need it. This drink is sure to add some excitement to your morning with no added calories or sugar.

"A good laugh and a long sleep are the best cures in the doctor's book." *Irish Proverb*

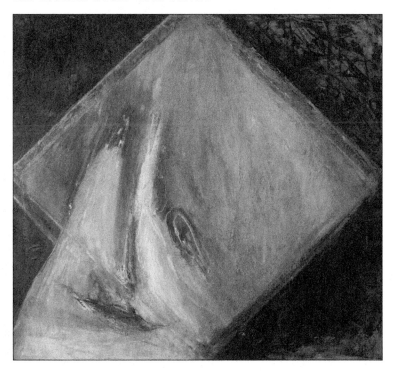

"Sleep is the best meditation." *Dalai Lama*

Zeven Zurprising Facts About Zleep

"Sleep is a symptom of caffeine deprivation." *Anonymous*

Studies show that...

- Sleep makes you smarter
- Sleep helps you lose fat
- Sleep improves your athletic performance
- Sleep reduces stress
- Sleeping helps you live longer
- Sleep makes you more creative
- Sleep puts you in a good mood

"I love sleep. My life has the tendency to fall apart when I'm awake, you know?" *Ernest Hemingway*

So be happy and choose to snooze!

"The best bridge between despair and hope is a good night's sleep." *E. Joseph Crossman*

"I'm not a very good sleeper. But you know what? I'm willing to put in a few extra hours every day to get better. That's just the kind of hard worker I am." *Jarod Kintz*

What comes after the end?

"Be open to what comes next for you. You may be heading in one direction and then life brings you another that might be a good thing." *Natalie Cane*

Did you think you had come to the end? In the Swedish alphabet, Z is followed by three more letters, Å, Ä and Ö. If you feel down because something is ending, it's a good idea to remind yourself that there is always more to come. What looks like the end might actually be the beginning of something we didn't see coming before — something new, something better. When we open ourselves up to surprise and positivity, the world opens itself up to us...

"We must let go of the life we have planned, so as to accept the one that is waiting for us." *Joseph Campbell*

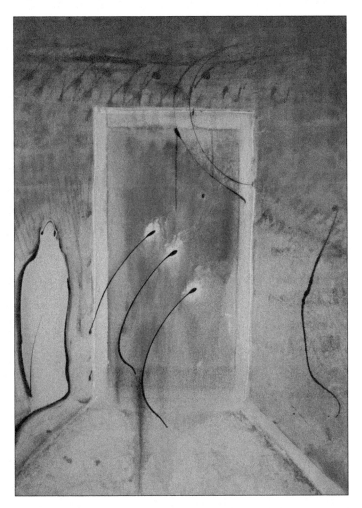

"My therapist told me the way to achieve true innner peace is to finish what I start. So far, I have finished two bags of M&Ms and chocolate cake. I feel better already." *Dave Barry*

Ok! Ak!

— *Go!* —

"Man cannot discover new oceans unless he has the courage to lose sight of the shore." *Andre Gide*

Always keep on going. When you reach your goal, say, Next! If you fail, say Next! Don't settle for mediocracy. Go for it! Travel, explore, investigate, question! Fill your life with enthusiasm and things that push you forward.

"Keep on going and the chances are you will stumble on something, perhaps when you are least expecting it. I have never heard of anyone stumbling on something sitting down." *Charles Kettering*

"The real journey of discovery is not to search for new landscape, but to have new eyes." *Marcel Proust*

"The first step toward changing the world is to change our vision of the world and our place in it."
Arianna Huffington

Kladdkaka

Gluten Free, low on sugar and absolutely incredible!

Ingredients:
3 eggs
1.5 cups sugar
½ tsp salt
1 tsp vanilla extract
5 tbsp unsweetened cocoa powder
2 tsp strong coffee
½ cup whole milk
150 g melted butter

Make it happen!
1. Whisk the eggs and sugar together until they have a nice airiness about them.
2. Gently stir in salt, vanilla, cocoa and flour until uniform in color and consistency.
3. Gently mix in coffee, milk and butter.
4. Pour mix into a buttered, round pie dish.

Bake!
Set the oven to 350 F and bake for 30-35 minutes
The cake is ready when it's just a little gooey, but not wet.

Enjoy!
Serve room temperature or chilled with some whipped cream, berries, bananas or peaches.

Älska

Love

"Love is an act of endless forgiveness,
a tender look which becomes a habit."
Peter Ustinov

Love is romantic! Love is familial!
Love is hopefully in everything we do!

To be loving in how we speak is good — to be loving
in how we act is even better. Often, it's as simple as
getting up and greeting somebody happily when they
enter the room, paying attention to your friend rather
than your phone or bringing your coworker their
favorite coffee drink every now and again.

"If you would be loved, love and be loveable."
Benjamin Franklin

"We waste time looking for the perfect lover, instead of creating the perfect love." *Tom Robbins*

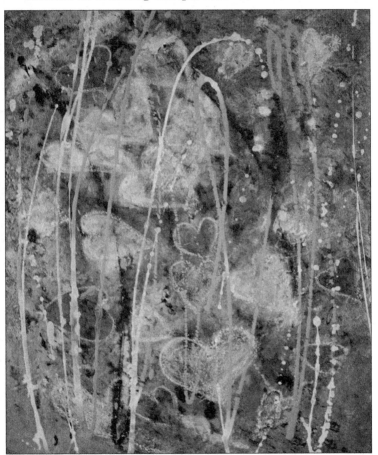

"We must not, in trying to think about how we can make a big difference, ignore the small daily differences we can make which, over time, add up to big differences that we often cannot foresee."
Marian Wright Edelman

Chokladbollar

Egg & Gluten free, No-Bake, Unbelievably Addictive!

Ingredients:
100g room temp. butter
1 tbsp cocoa powder
4 tbsp sugar
1.25 cups rolled oatmeal
1 tbsp strong coffee

Toppings:
Pearl sugar
Coconut
Walnuts
Anything you like!

Make it happen!
Thoroughly mix all the ingredients (not toppings) in a bowl. Roll bite-size balls of the mix with your hands and place upon a plate. Roll the balls around in the toppings of your choice. Refrigerate for at least 30 minutes.

Enjoy!
Eat up! There's no wrong way to enjoy a chokladboll.

Island

"Our ancient experience confirms at every point that everything is linked together, everything is inseparable." *Dalai Lama XIV*

It's easy to get caught up in the illusion of separation when we are stressed out. Many of us seem to forget that we're even on the same planet.

"We are like islands in the sea, separate on the surface but connected in the deep."
William James

It helps to remind ourselves that, just like islands, we are all connected to one another — sometimes you just have to go a little deeper to see that.

"We cannot live only for ourselves. A thousand fibers connect us with our fellow men; and among those fibers, as sympathetic threads, our actions run as causes, and they come back to us as effects."
Herman Melville

If more people took the time to sit down and get to know each other through Fika, we could learn to see that we are all connected, and none of us are alone.

"Those who see the cosmic perspective as a depressing outlook, they really need to reassess how they think about the world. Because when I look up in the universe, I know I'm small but I'm also big. I'm big because I'm connected to the universe, and the universe is connected to me." *Neil deGrasse Tyson*

Schackrutor

Egg free, beautiful and absolutely delicious.

"Sometimes me think, what is friend? And then me say a friend is someone to share last cookie with." *Cookie Monster*

General Ingredients:
2.25 cups flour
½ cup sugar
½ tsp salt
200g room temp. butter

White:
1.5 tsp vanilla extract
(the white color is best
achieved with 2tsp vanilla
sugar, but vanilla extract
yields a similar taste)

Brown:
2 tbsp cocoa powder

Make it happen!
Mix the "general ingredients" in a bowl. Separate the
dough into two equal amounts and place into separate
bowls. Add "white" and "brown" ingredients to separate

Take the white dough and split it into two. Work each half
into a long, rectangular loaf about 8-10 inches. Repeat this
step with the brown half.

Once you have four little loaves, stack them 2x2 to give the
"checkerboard" effect. It's a good idea to push gently on
each side of the combined loaf to make sure the different
colors stick together through baking. Cut the cookies into
½ - ¾ inch slices and place on a baking sheet.

Bake!
350 F for 10-12 minutes. Cookies should be soft, not mushy.

Enjoy!
Just eat up, and remember to share!

Åsa Katarina

After teaching Law at the university of Stockholm, working as a consultant with executives at major companies like Ericsson and Volvo and having art shows all over the world, Åsa Filippa moved to Santa Barbara where she is living her dream of writing, painting and enjoying daily Fikas with her coauthor and son.

Émile

Having recently graduated from the University of California Santa Barbara, where he served as the Editor in Chief of his university's nationally ranked newspaper and earned straight As, Émile now lives in Santa Barbara and still can't believe that he gets to call tasting coffee, speaking and writing his job.

CPSIA information can be obtained
at www.ICGtesting.com
Printed in the USA
BVOW05s0816201217
503123BV00041B/373/P